Educational Activities

OUR WORLD

Illustrations by Belinda Willson

ISBN: 1 86476 234 9

Copyright © Axiom Publishing, 2003.
Unit 2, 1 Union Street, Stepney, South Australia, 5069.

This book is copyright. Apart from any fair dealing for the purpose of private study, research, criticism or review, as permitted under the Copyright Act, no part may be reproduced by any process without written permission.
Enquiries should be made to the publisher.
www.axiomdistributors.com.au

Printed in Malaysia

DAY AND NIGHT

Draw the other half of these pictures. Which of these would you see in the sky at night? Colour them yellow

Moon

Cloud

Sun

Star

SPORTS

Look at the words below. Draw a line from each sport to the place it is played. Circle the sport in the picture.

Football	Snow
Skiing	Dart Board
Swimming	Pool
Tennis	Court
Darts	Ground

TRANSPORT

How do you travel?
Colour the transport you have used before.

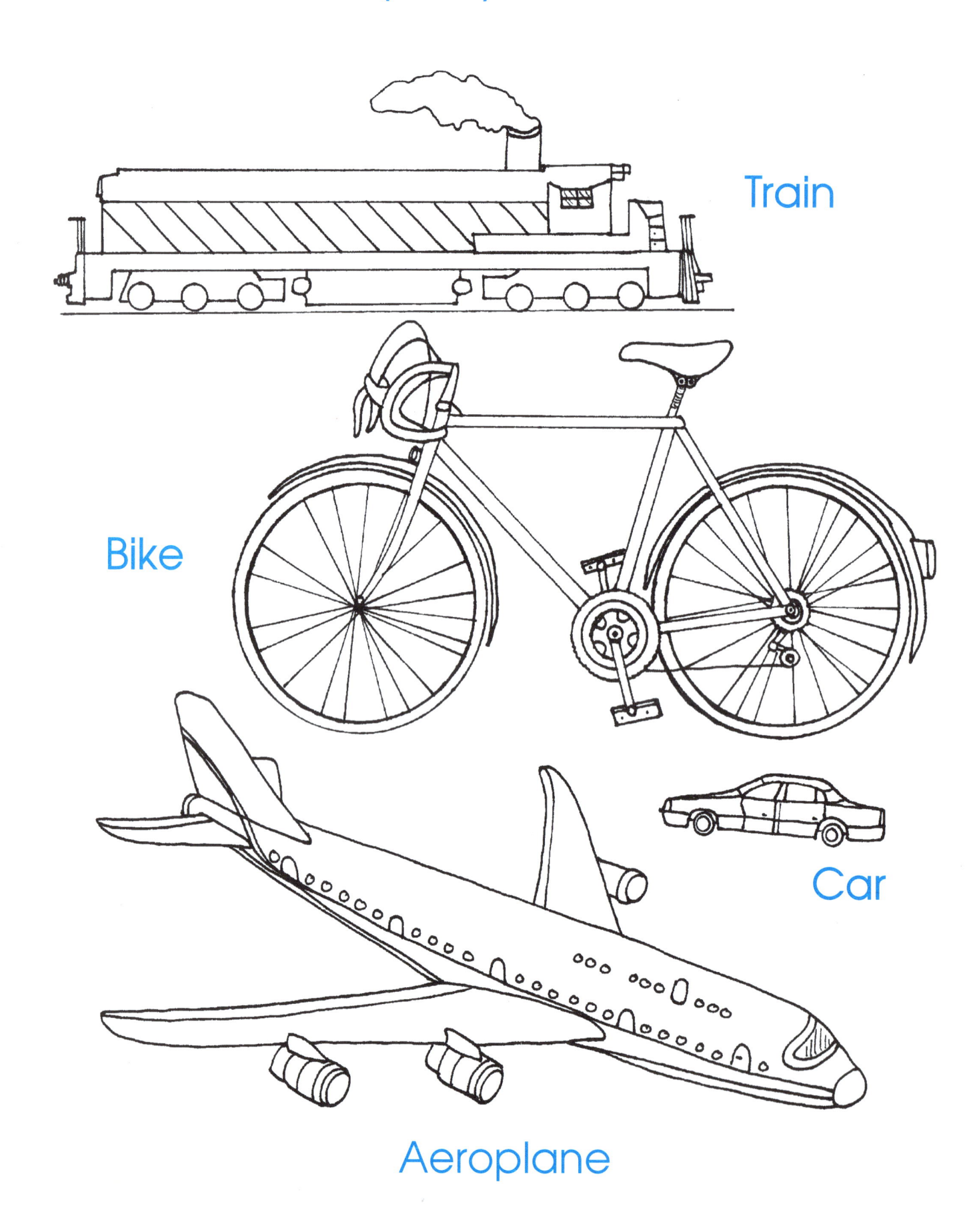

Train

Bike

Car

Aeroplane

RECYCLING

Sam and Amanda are concerned about their environment. They have collected items from their home to recycle. Count the number of items each child is recycling and write the answers on their Shirts. Now write the items alphabetically on Sam and Amanda's list.

Recycling list in alphabetical order

Sam

tin cans
jars
milk cartons
drink bottles
newspapers

Amanda

CIRCLE THE WORDS

Dd diver DIVER

Circle the words that relate to a diver

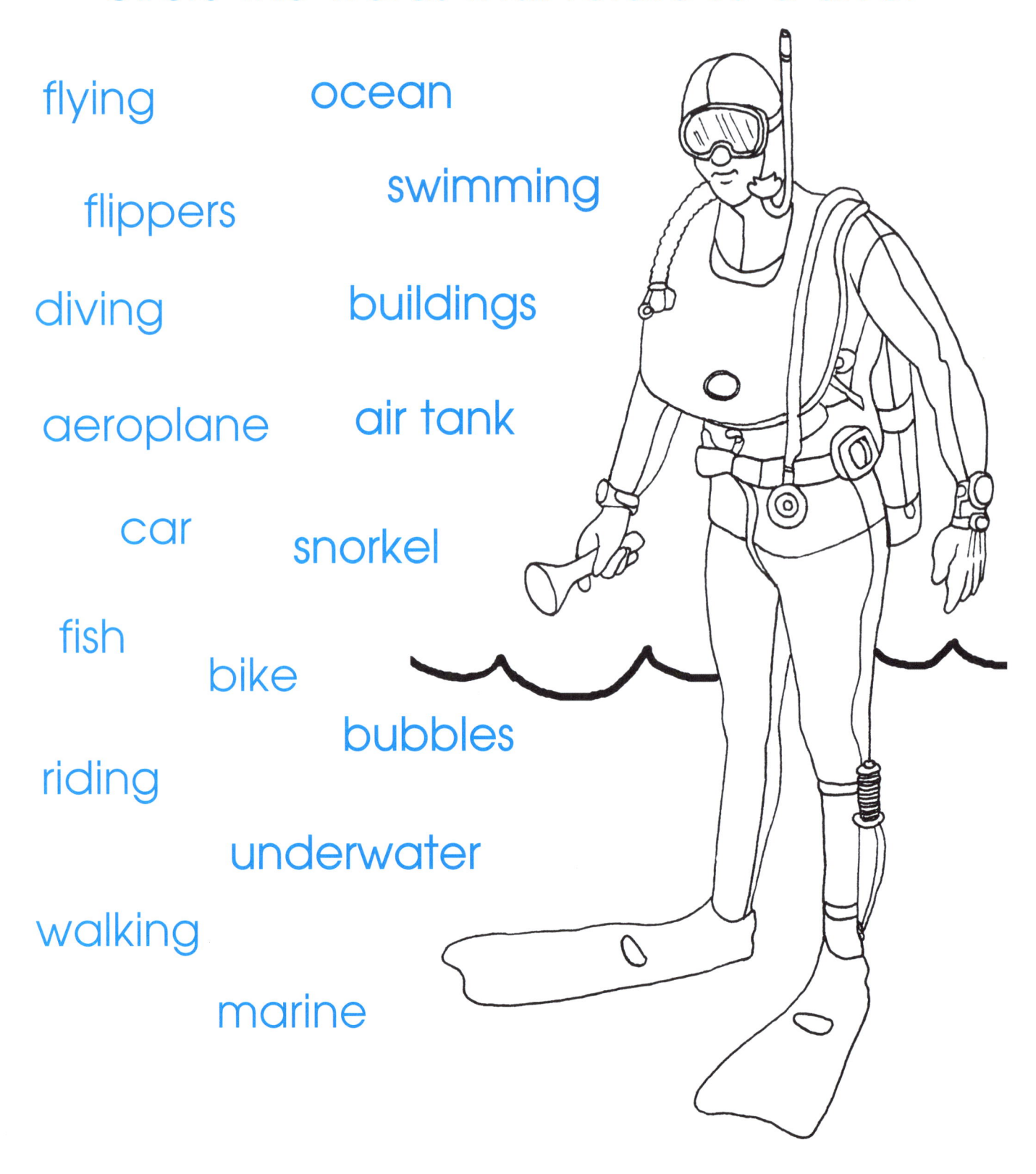

flying

ocean

flippers

swimming

diving

buildings

aeroplane

air tank

car

snorkel

fish

bike

bubbles

riding

underwater

walking

marine

UNIVERSE

A telescope is used to look at the night sky.

How many of each can you count?

☆ =   ◯ =   ☽ =

☄ =   🚀 =

FOLLOW THE MAZE

Follow the path through the maze to find on which planet the spaceman will land his spaceship. Then write the numbers 1 to 9 inside the planets from the smallest to the largest.

Start

Neptune

Earth

Venus

Mars

Jupiter

Uranus

Mercury

Pluto

Saturn

FRUIT

Draw a line from the objects to the correct number.

Apples

Banana

Cherries

Apricots

1 one

2 two

3 three

4 four

5 five

WHAT IS THE DIFFERENCE

Which squirrel is different? Colour it.

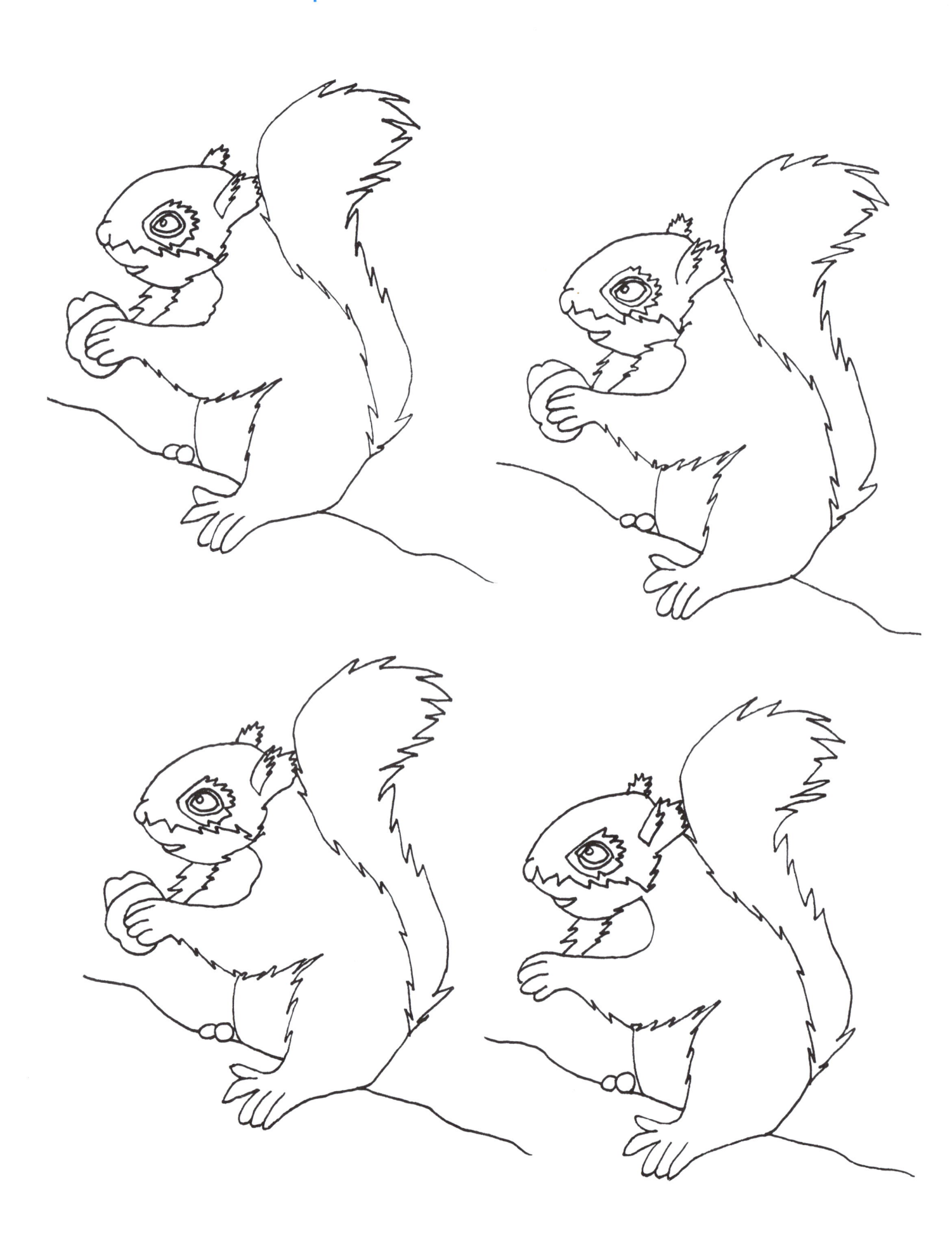

WINTER

Read these sentences to fill in the missing words below.
This bear lives in the mountains of Canada.
During winter bears sleep in their den to keep warm because it is very very cold.
This is called hibernating.
When spring arrives the bear wakes up.

This _____ lives in the mountains of Canada.
During winter bears _____ in their _____,
to keep warm because it is very very _____.
This is called _____.
When spring arrives the _____ wakes ___.

NUMBER SKILLS

Which leaf will this butterfly land on to lay its eggs? Do the sums on the leaves and match the answers to the number on the butterfly. Colour the correct leaf green.

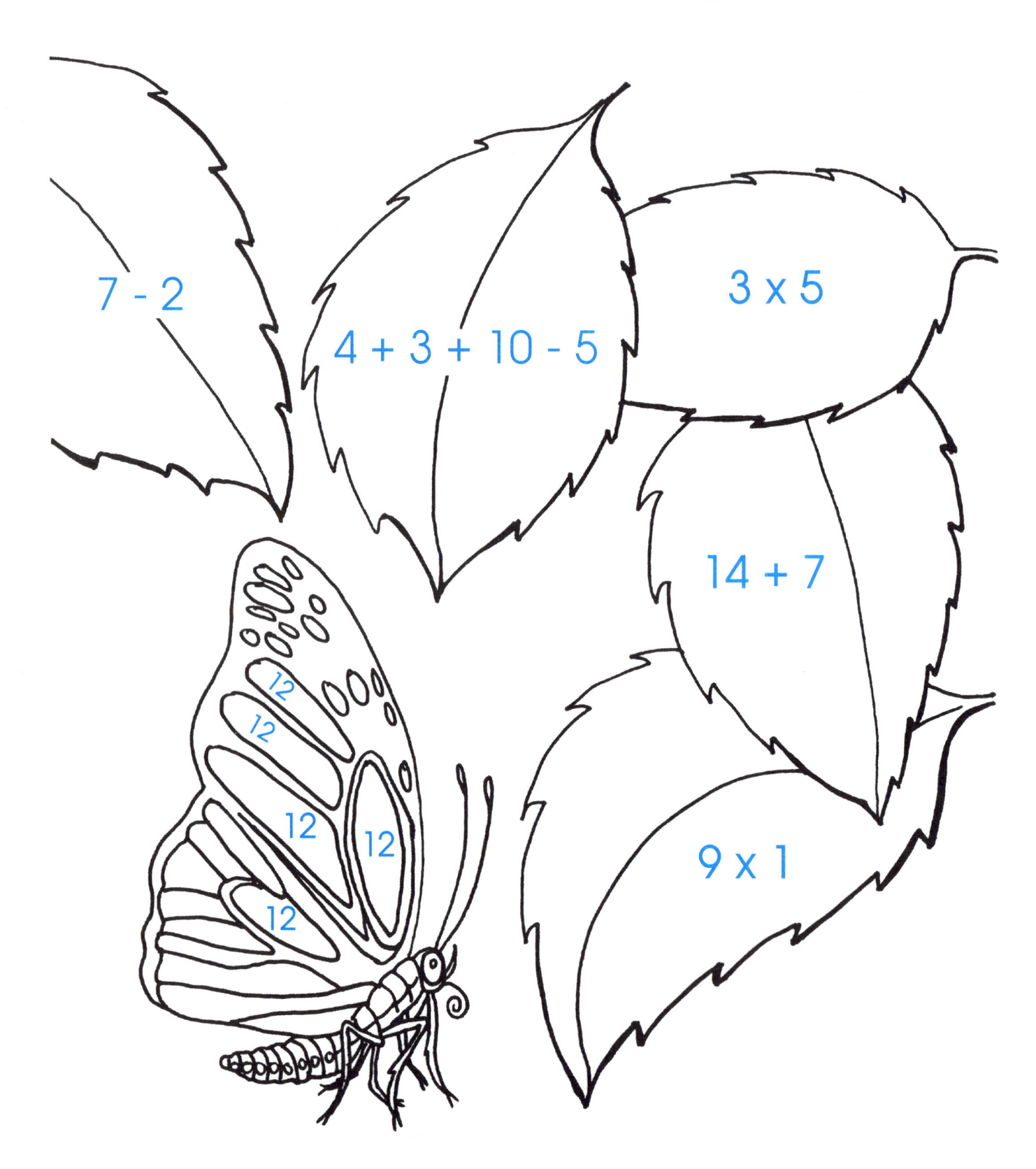

7 - 2

4 + 3 + 10 - 5

3 x 5

14 + 7

9 x 1

12
12
12
12
12

CAMPING

Find and colour

Find and colour:

Sleeping bag = green.

Tent = red.

Drink container = yellow.

Lamp = blue

Fire = orange

DRAW AND COUNT

These animals are called Hamsters. Many people keep them as cuddly pets. This mother hamster has two babies. Draw 3 more, how many does she have now?

LETTER SKILLS

Unscramble the word to find out where this orangutan lives.

UEJNGL _____

BIRD WATCHING

Binoculars can be used for bird watching. Can you spot:

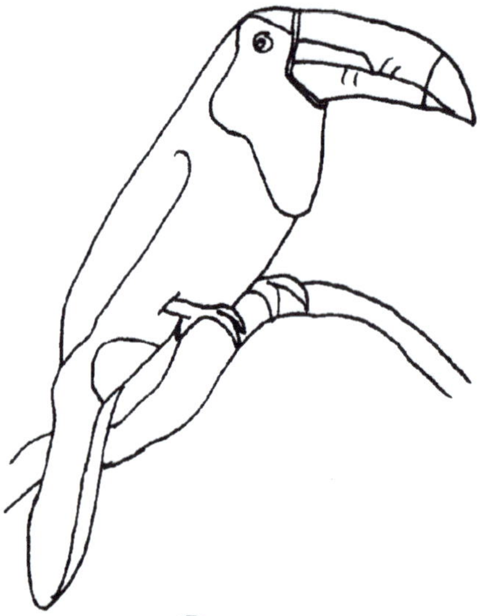

- a flock of birds, circle them.

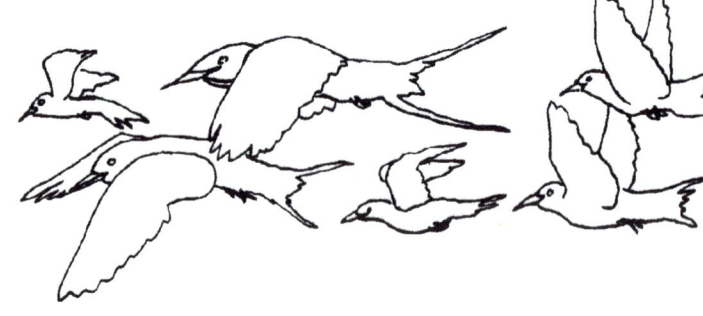

- a bird with a long beak, colour it red, yellow and green.

- 2 parrots, colour them blue and purple.

- a creature that is not a bird, colour it brown.

LETTER SKILLS

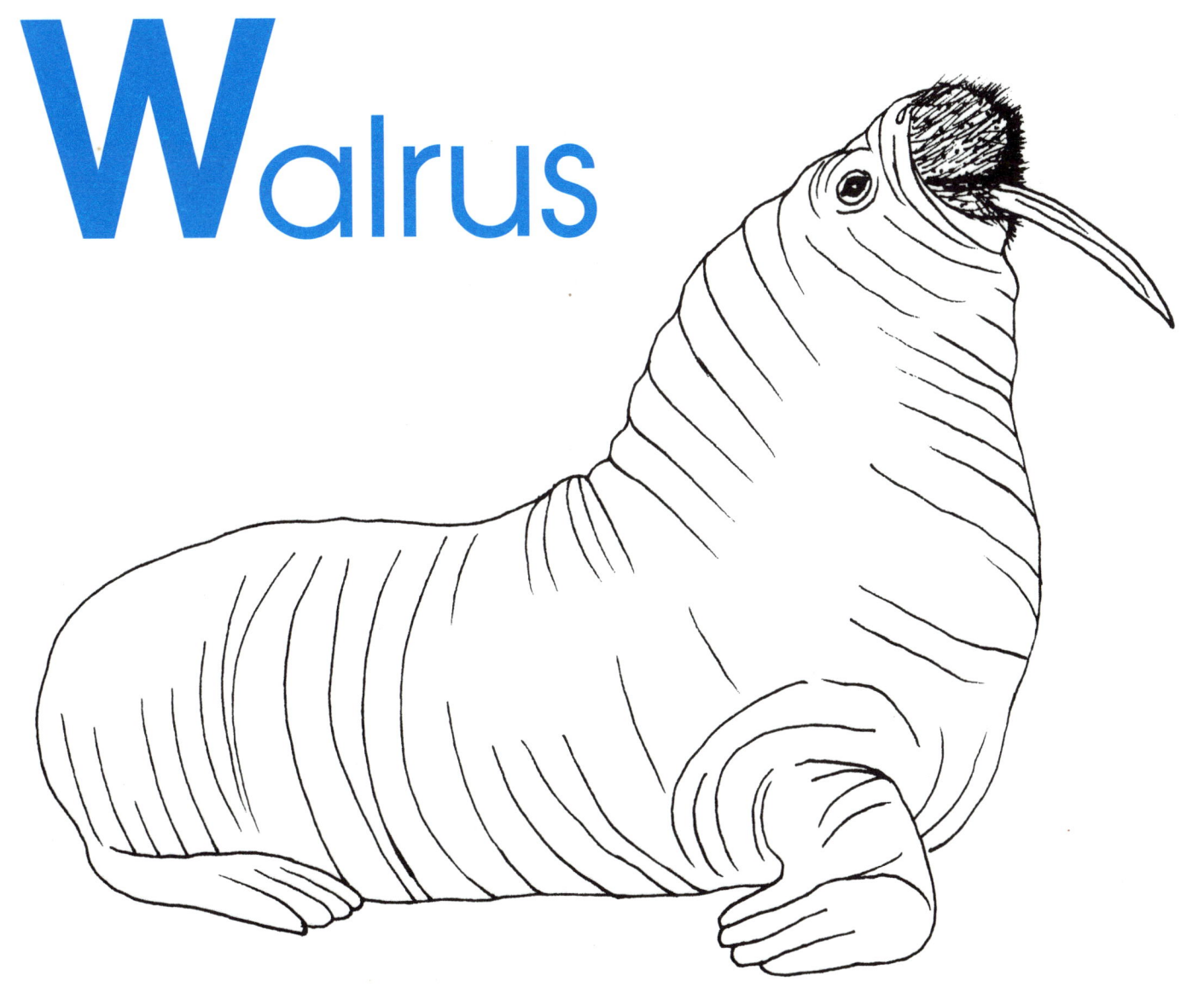

Walrus

Circle the words that begin with w.

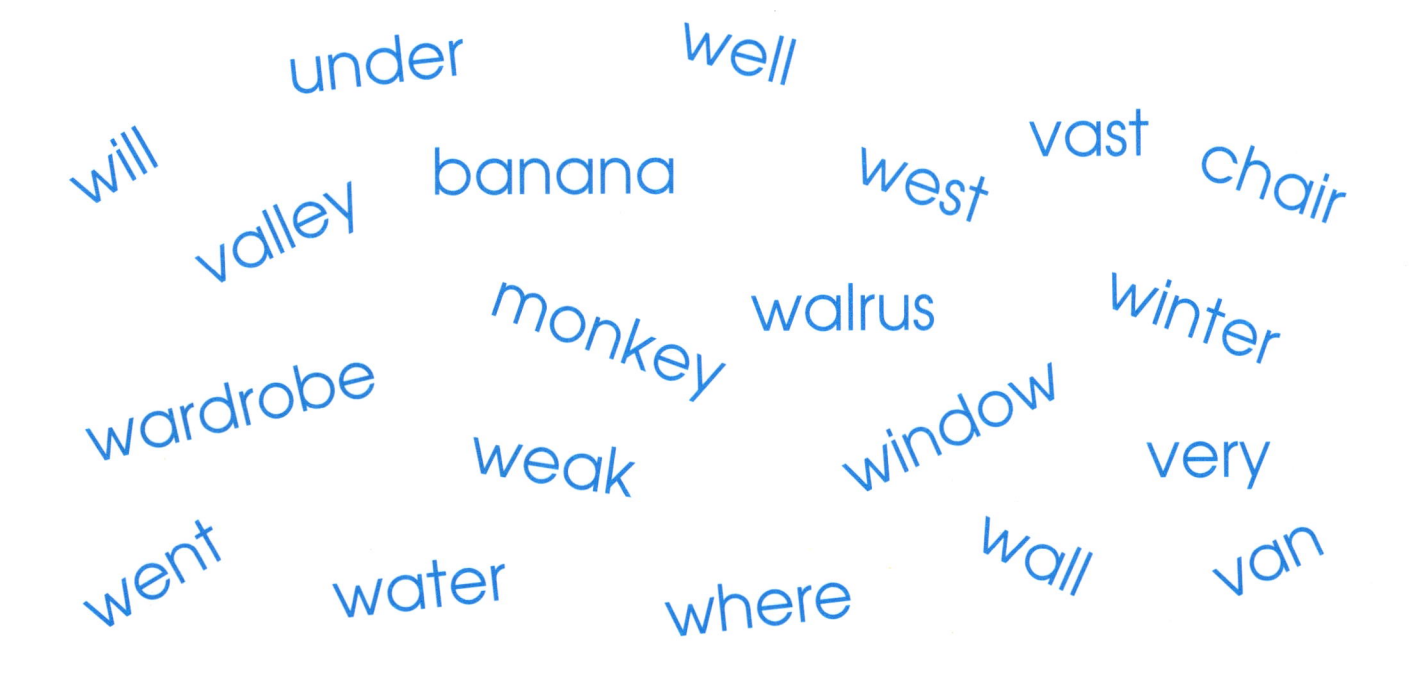

under   well

will   valley   banana   west   vast   chair

monkey   walrus   winter

wardrobe   weak   window   very

went   water   where   wall   van

ANIMAL SOUNDS

Draw a line from the animal to the sound that it makes.

Meow   Cheep   Woof   Ba Ba

WORD SEARCH

Look at these pictures and find them in the word puzzle.

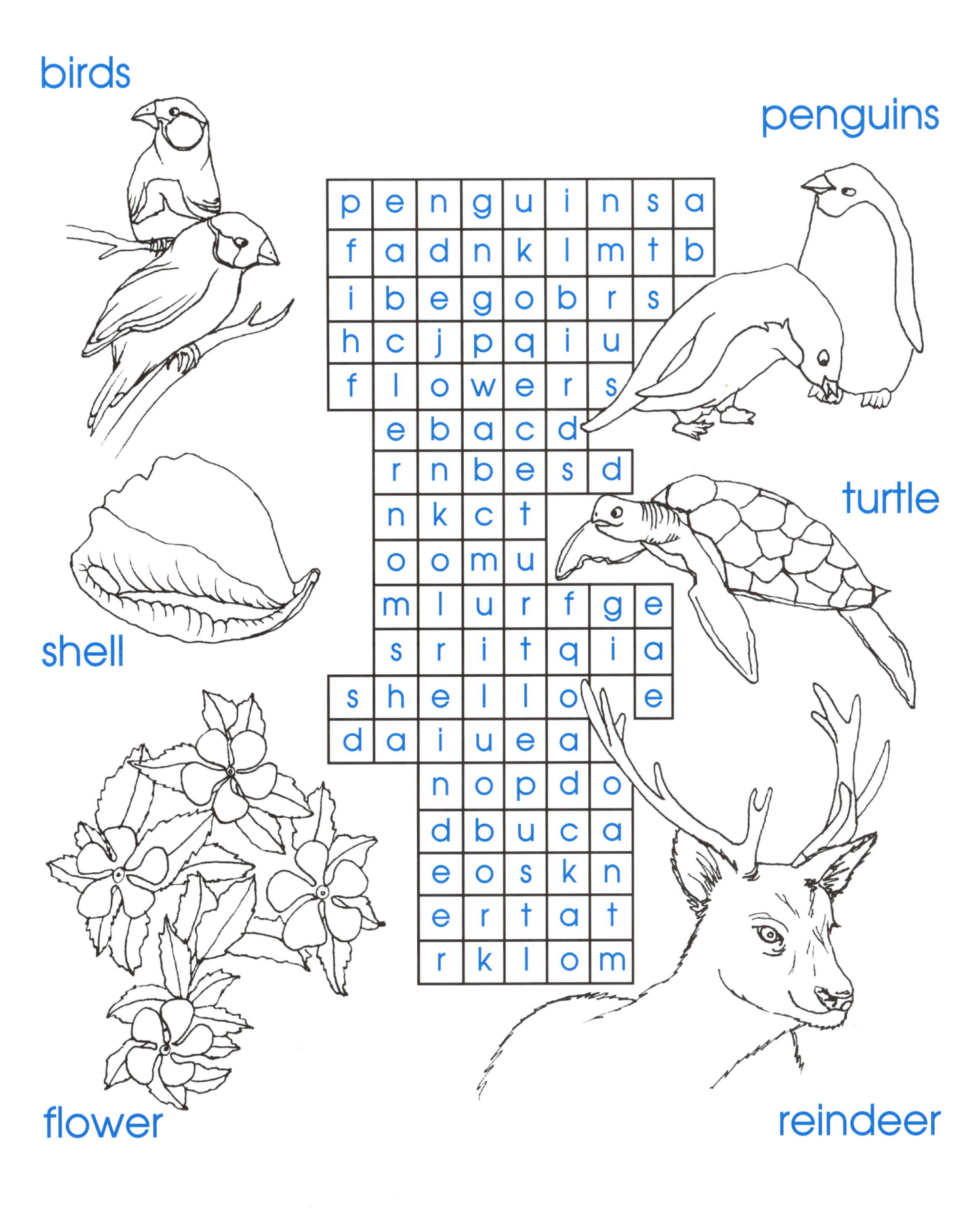

birds

penguins

p	e	n	g	u	i	n	s	a
f	a	d	n	k	l	m	t	b
i	b	e	g	o	b	r	s	
h	c	j	p	q	i	u		
f	l	o	w	e	r	s		
	e	b	a	c	d			
	r	n	b	e	s	d		
	n	k	c	t				
	o	o	m	u				
	m	l	u	r	f	g	e	
	s	r	i	t	q	i	a	
	s	h	e	l	l	o		
	d	a	i	u	e	a	e	
	n	o	p	d	o			
	d	b	u	c	a			
	e	o	s	k	n			
	e	r	t	a	t			
	r	k	l	o	m			

turtle

shell

flower

reindeer

LETTER SKILLS

P p

Pigeon p_____

LETTER SKILLS

Can you work out how these words fit into the puzzle.

raccoon

cockatoo

armadillo

beaver

MISSING PARTS

Look at these pictures carefully. Draw what is missing on both animals. Here is a clue:
A giraffe has 4 legs. An elephant has a very long nose called a trunk.

AARDVARK

How many ants and termites will the Aardvark eat. Do the sum to find out. Then cross out or draw more ants to make that number.

6 + 2 - 1 =   ants

DRAWING

The golden lion tamarin lives in a rainforest. Draw leaves and trees to give this monkey his right home.

LETTERING SKILLS

Look at the words and colour them according to the rhyming words.

rat
sold
mat
big
bold
gold
bold
rug
egg told

If the word rhymes with cat colour it blue.
If the word rhymes with old colour it green.
If the word rhymes with pig colour it orange.
If the word rhymes with peg colour it red.
If the word rhymes with bug colour it yellow.

Parrots
Parrots

IN THE GARDEN

Count the snails and write your answer in the small leaf. Colour 2 snails red, 2 yellow, 4 blue and 3 orange.

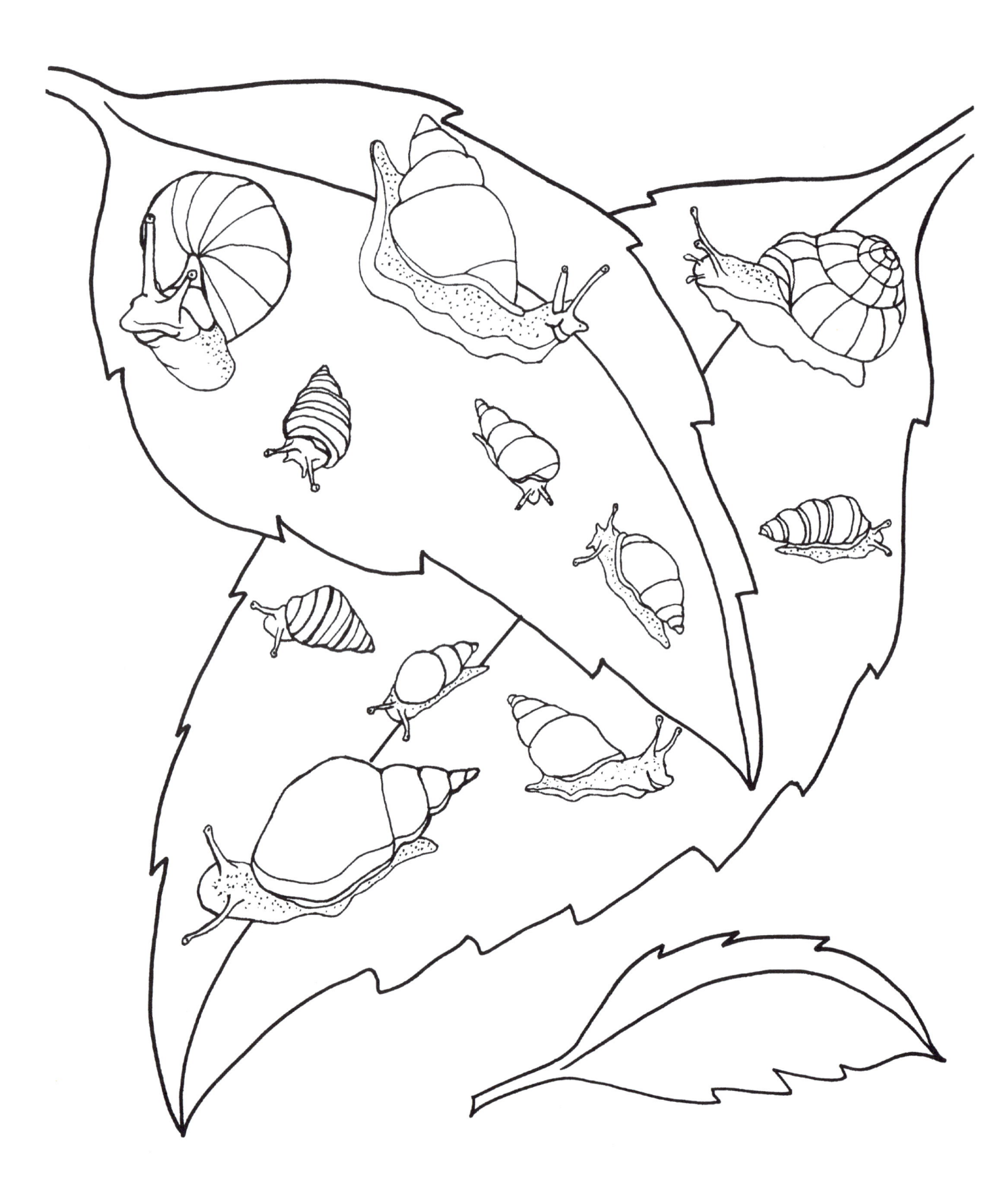

LETTER SKILLS

F f   Flying Fox

Fill in the correct words

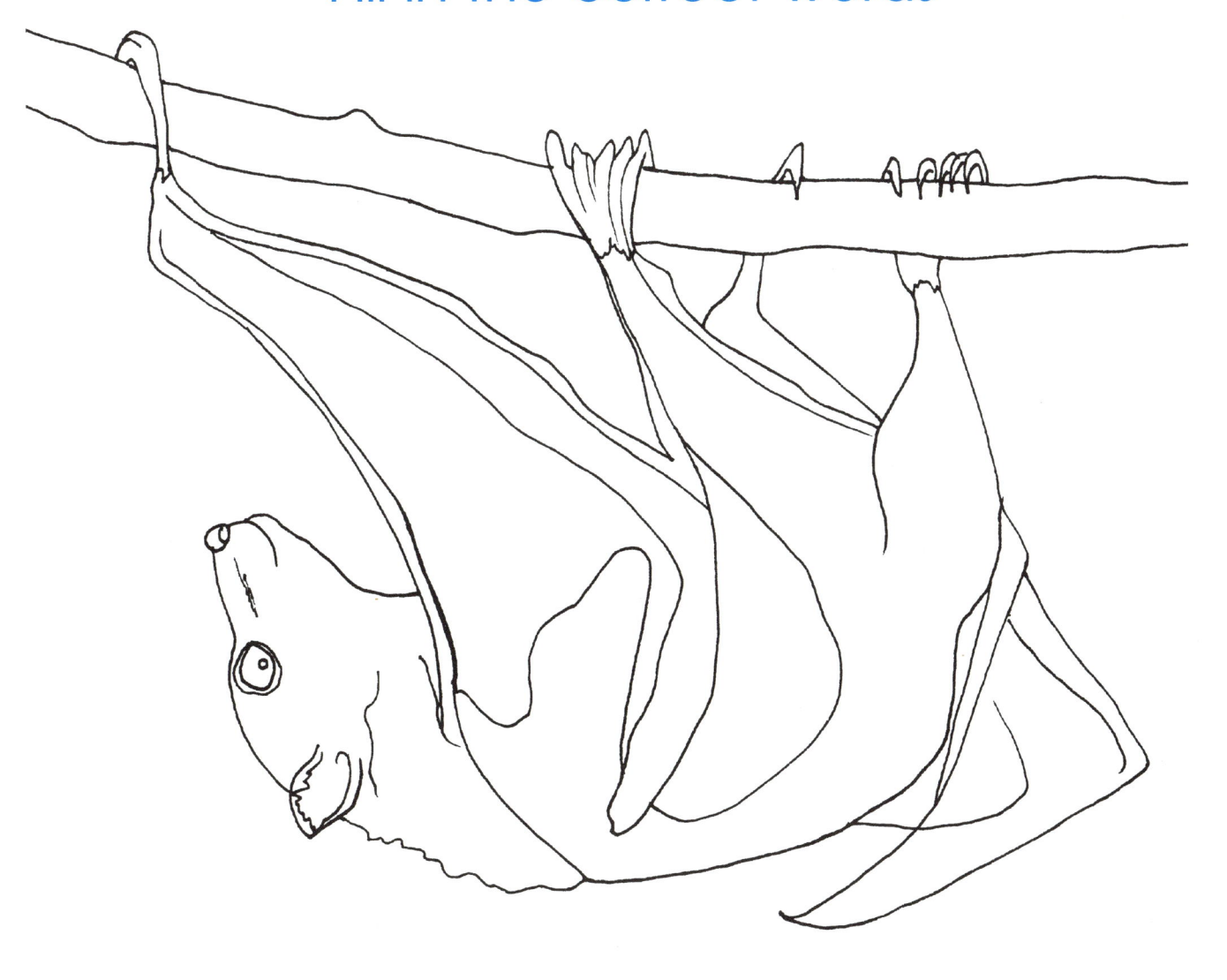

This flying fox is _____ on the branch.

standing tall,
hanging upside down
sitting down

POSSUMS

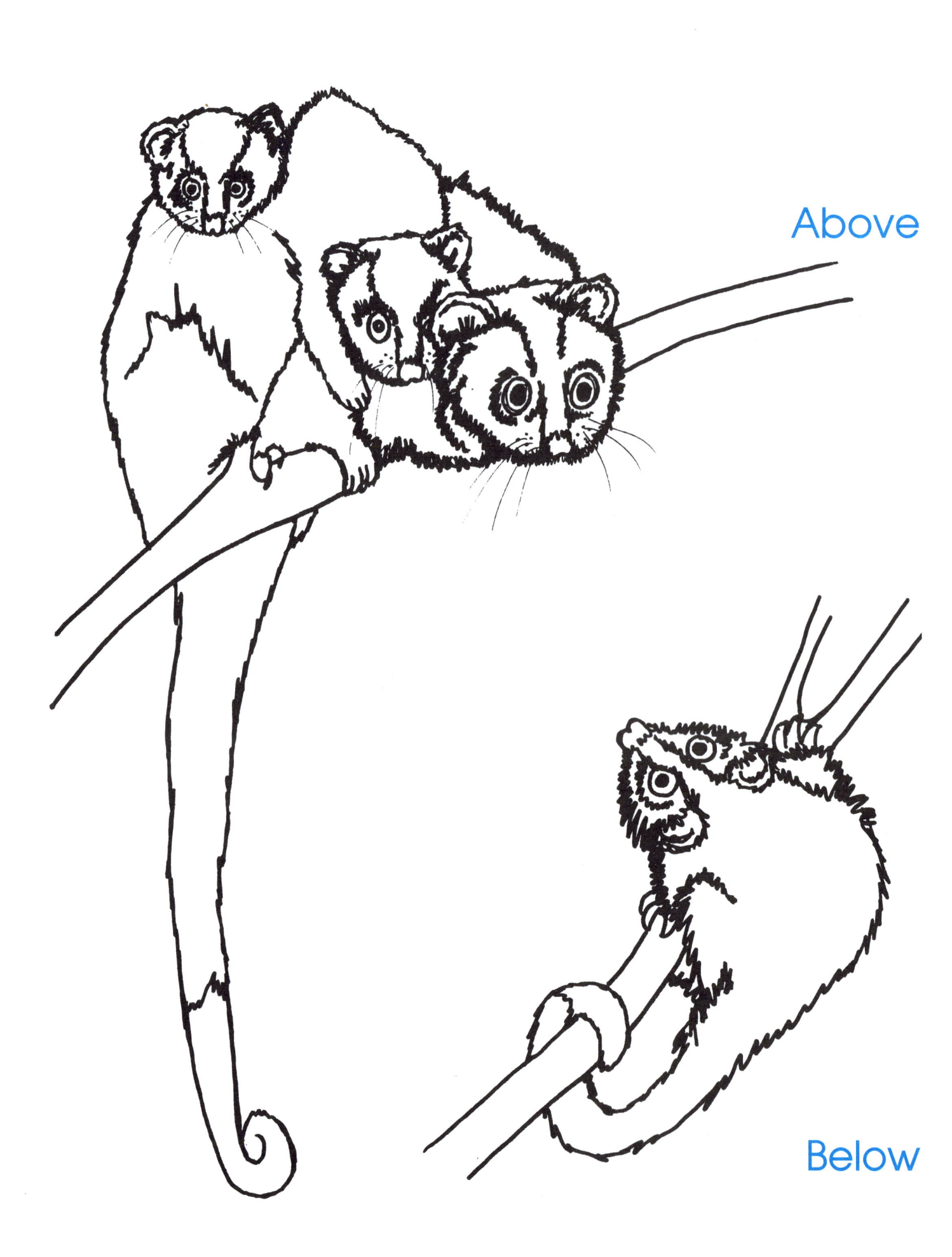

Above

Below

MIX AND MATCH

Look at these parts of animals and draw a line to the matching word.

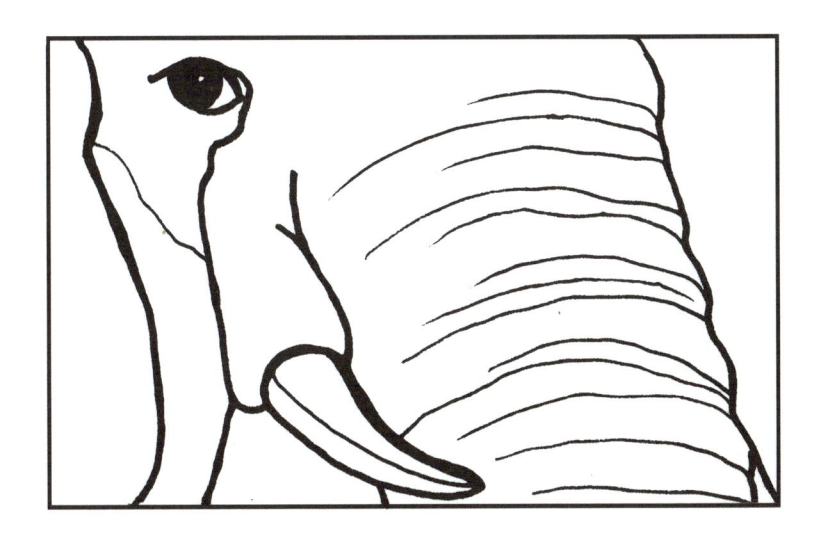

fish

butterfly

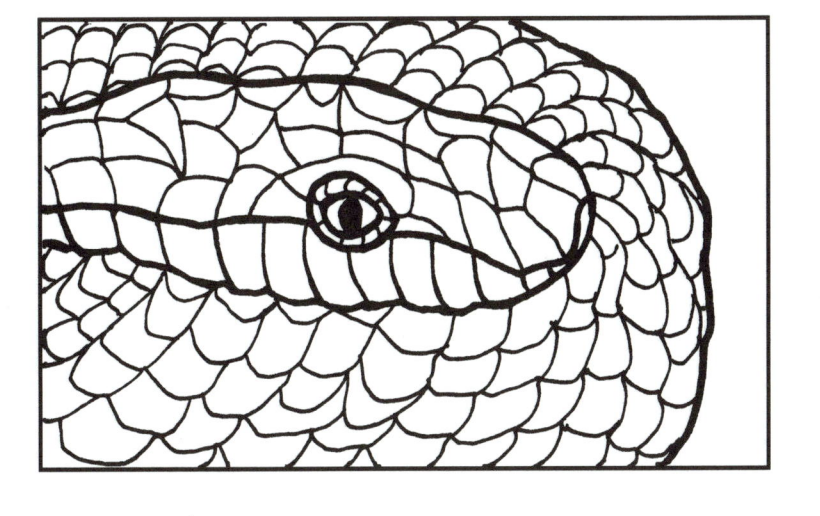

elephant

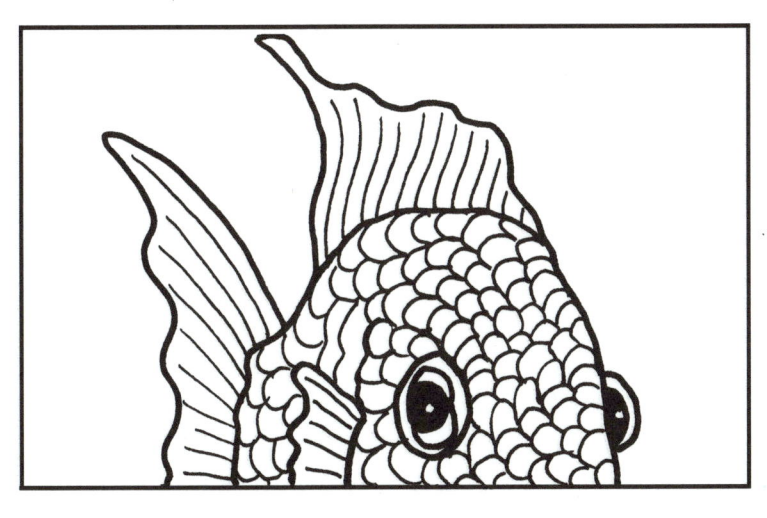

horse

snake

NUMBER SKILLS

Do the sums and join the answers to the turtle with same number.

2 + 4 =

2 + 2 + 2 =

5 x 2 =

3 x 3 =

10 - 4 =

3 x 2 =

10 - 1 =

6 + 3 =

10

6

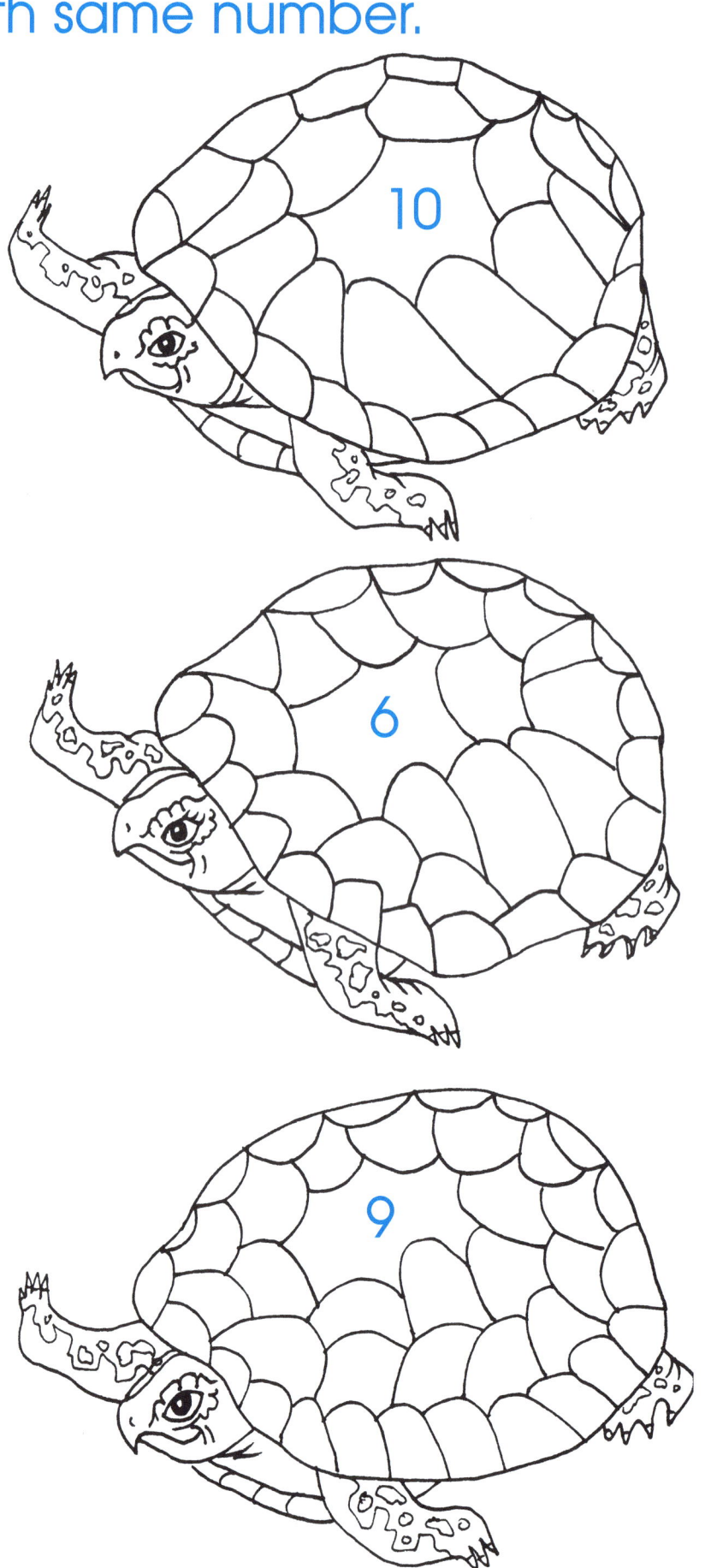

9

MAZE

Billy is going to the beach. He needs to protect himself from the hot sun. Help him find his way to the sun-safe items.

Sun Cream

NUMBER SKILLS

How many garden tools can you count? Write answer inside the flower.